MW00745074

I Sing In Silence

I Sing
In Silence

THE POETRY OF

Robyn
Taradash

GRANNY APPLE PUBLISHING LLC SARASOTA, FLORIDA

I Sing in Silence:

The Poetry of Robyn Taradash

This book is an original work of original poetry written by Robyn Taradash.

Cover Art and Inside Page Art on page 1 and 7 from
Original Oil on Canvas "Agony and the Lily" by Karin Zukowski
Cover and Interior Graphic Design: Miguel Valcarcel, Visual Media Arts

Published by
Granny Apple Publishing, LLC, Sarasota, FL
www.grannyapplepublishing.com

Partial proceeds from the sale of this book are being donated to The National Multiple Sclerosis Society. Additional donations to the Society can be made directly on the Robyn Taradash: I Sing in Silence Fund Page at www.nationalmssociety.org

Cataloging-in-Publication Data

Taradash, Estelle

I Sing in Silence: The Poetry of Robyn Taradash / by Robyn Taradash

Granny Apple Publishing LLC trade pbk. Ed.

Library of Congress Control Number: 2012931337

PAPERBACK ISBN: 0983130590

PAPERBACK EAN-13: 978-0-9831305-9-8

In Loving Memory of Robyn

Dear Winnie —

Enjoy the Road

& the Pictures

E Kelly

© KARIZU

Foreword

This book of poems was written by Robyn Taradash when she was in her high school and college years. She experienced some symptoms as early as age 16, and was diagnosed with Multiple Sclerosis at age 18. She was accepted at Hofstra University in Hempstead, New York, where she majored in English and maintained a very high academic average. She graduated Magna Cum Laude and received permanent certification for teaching.

She accepted a position as an English teacher at Northport High School in Long Island where she was very successful and her work in the English Department was highly acclaimed. After completing just one semester, however, her disabilities exacerbated. Her walking became extremely labored and the resulting stress caused her to resign and come home.

These poems reflect a period in Robyn's life when the average teenager feels indestructible and unassailable. But due to her limited physical abilities, Robyn felt isolated, lonely, vulnerable and understandably frightened of what the future had in store for her.

She suffered with the disease until she was fifty-six years old. Near the end of her short life, she became totally bedridden and was almost blind. After a lifetime of suffering, Robyn died a tragic death. She endured several brain seizures and could no longer be cared for at home. Her last five months were spent in a nursing home.

It was discovered that one of the aides at the nursing home was responsible for an injury that inflicted "blunt force trauma" to the head. It was ruled a homicide by the investigating police who had been alerted by Children & Families Services that this was a case of abuse. The institution tried to cover up the situation by stating that Robyn had become unresponsive from not eating and was jaundiced and they determined the only solution was to send her to the hospital. At the hospital, X-rays taken revealed that her brain was hemorrhaging. She passed away three days later.

These poems are Robyn's legacy.

~ Estelle Taradash

There is no one here now,

No one to help me drink

The left-over wine

Of grey yesterdays

And blue tomorrows.

Tangled here in silken cobwebs

Of drifting clouds,

I Sing In Silence

Caged Bird

Beyond your reach the mountain tops
Where only eagles soar
Beyond your reach the open skies
Above the ocean's roar.

You cannot even hitch a ride
Upon a passing breeze
Cannot jump from branch to branch
and play among the trees.

Cannot tease the daisies
As they comb their long white hair
Or brush against the velvet gowns
That Petunias always wear.

Just watch the caterpillar
As he accordians his way
To where caterpillars go
When they want to dance and play.

Just sit and sing a quiet song
As blue-bells gently ring
For little Robyn cannot fly
She has a broken wing.

~ Aunt Lillian

Contents

Foreword 8
   I Sing in Silence
   Caged Bird
Family 13
Change 21
Friendship 27
The Seasons 35
Love 43
Love Lost 59
Loneliness 69
Despair 75
Hope 87
Death 95
Au Revoir 99
Afterword 103
   Summer of '42 in '71
   How's My Little Girl?
   Remembering Robyn
The Puzzle 110
The List 111

Family

To my Mom and Dad

You are my strength

When I am weak

You are my warmth

When winds blow cold

You are everything

I could ever ask for

You make me smile when I am sad

You give me courage

When there is none

Most of all you forgive

And that is the essence of Love.

To Great Parents

You were always there when I needed you

To give me hope when I had none

To help me cope

When I lost the sun

You gathered the pieces when they broke

Washed my pants when they were soaked

I know it's been a task

Getting through my mask

Accepting my pain

Withstanding my strain

Yes - We've all been hurt

But somehow,

Love heals all —

Even when it seems like a tough haul

Dad

You are the Greatest Father

I could have asked for –

You showed me kindness

When I didn't deserve it

You gave me confidence

When I had none

You dried my tears (and there were many)

You eased my fears

You've always understood

When I couldn't do something

And gave me comfort when I was alone

Although we argued

You always forgave me

And in short, taught me

The meaning of Love.

Daddy

Oh, Daddy, you never let
The music in your life.
You listened only
To dark news
Of bloody murder
And stormy weather.
You never saw
Rainbows in the clouds
Or sunshine in the wind.
And oh, Daddy,
Maybe that is why
You only saw my pain
And not my joy.
You never knew
That life is filled
Not only with tears,
But also with laughter.
Oh, Daddy, before you go,
See my joy,
Tell me I did the best I could
With what I had.
And smile for me, Daddy—
it's not really all that bad,
Is it?

Hidden Hope

So alone
Filled with gnawing pain
That comes with empty spaces ...
Who left them?
Was it the boy who went
When he saw the way I was?
Was it my mother
Who brushed me aside
To seek her freedom?
(That's expected, I guess.)
Maybe it was the job I lost
When I wasn't good enough.
Or perhaps my sister left a hole—
Too busy to talk these days—
Or could it have been the rain
That soaked the grounds
And wouldn't let me walk
(The little I can, anyway).
Can you fill an empty space
Or mend the broken glass?
I wait and watch the game—
The Yankees lost today.

Strength

You do not like my darkness

Or so you say,

But take some time

To look beneath the shadows

And sit under an oak

To peer through empty spaces.

Echoes of our pain

Will form our chords

'Til we can sing in Harmony.

The Girl

The woman said the girl
Was only half a person,
For she did not have a job.
And the man
looked only at her legs
When He spoke to her,
Sighing at their lameness,
Their inability to carry her
To destined places.
He never saw the joy
In her eyes
Or learned what pleased her.
The woman said
The girl was not whole
And added up the cost
Of all the tolls.
Still, they thought they knew
THE GIRL
And made a good family
Until the girl
Cracked in little pieces
And
Left the two of them
ALONE.

Change

Moving Out

Tying up the loose ends of my life,
I pack old suitcases with memories,
Clean out drawers of withered letters.
Faded pictures of rainbow days
Mock the life that I have lived here.
Stark grey walls, emptied of their faces,
Recall dreams so long ago forgotten—
A frazzled rag doll on the bed,
With two missing button eyes,
Tossed aside in rueful anguish,
Is crying in her tattered dress.
Only one lone painting of a child,
Whose paint has dripped, remains.
As I pull down the shades,
Draw the curtains,
And lock the doors,
I leave one life
Only to begin another—
A tear-stained face.

That Day You Came to Visit: To Dean

That day you came to visit
We felt, amidst the nakedness of our souls,
Free of clutching, crawling vines,
The intensity of our passions
Dormant until then.
My body still feels your warm caresses,
My mind still knows the depth of your love,
My eyes still see the burning in your eyes,
And I still feel that tragic sense of loss
We both felt when time's hand
Struck our hearts.
That day you came to visit
There was God—
But again those massive vines
Clench your soul
And I am alone, searching the sky.

A Farewell to Adolescence: To Jon

I tried to grasp your hand to lead you

Past dark and fog-filled streets with me.

But you refused to comprehend

And never really knew at all.

Now the ivory lights are dimming

And it is time to go

Along the paths of ripened dreams.

In time I'll see you once again

With hair that's turned a smoky gray

Smiling that pretended smile

Unconscious of those pale pink days

Always smiling, never knowing—

A Lonely Night
To Jon

Walking past an all-night diner,

I can hear the moaning of a trumpet;

The smell of stale coffee lingers above—

A blood-stained road—remnants of

an auto-wreck—

The still wind speaks not even to the trees.

A stranger passes—I wonder where he roams.

I yearn to follow him, yet go on my way.

A silent star against an obscure sky

Leads me to the place where I must wait.

Friendship

Beginnings

Like a dream, a golden vision,

You came into my life,

And brought me sparkling skies,

A gifted note, a friendly call,

And we laughed,

Sharing breezy times—

Tired of losing so long,

We learned to begin again.

Seeds

I had really forgotten

Until

I saw your name imbedded

On the book you lent to me.

I tried to erase it

But somehow black ink

Just doesn't seem to disappear—

Then, after hiding the book,

I thought for sure

I had really forgotten

Until

I found the seeds

That you had planted.

Phone Calls

They were just phone calls,
Ordinary to some,
But you made each one so special,
So intimate, and we worked our magic
Together—
You wrapped your voice around my soul,
And caressed me with your words
So smoothly, so passionately, so tenderly.
You've made love to me with your words,
And that is why it's so hard to say goodbye,
Even if only for a day,
Because I love you so,
With every inch of my being—
Still, I'll relive your words,
Forever in my heart ...

More Phone Calls

They were just phone calls,
Made to say "Hello"
and
He didn't know
and
she didn't know
Just a little phone call
Could give me hope,
Could show me that all people
Aren't plastic.
Some people are really real—
Knowing I am thought of
Or accepted
For just a while, anyway,
Helps me through the day—
Call me tomorrow, please?

New Friend

You touched me in some special way, new friend,

Tho'I hardly know you,

But somehow I know

You're not a mystery,

But a kind and gentle soul.

Now I do not feel so empty,

And will not fear the drenching rains

Under trembling skies—

Until tomorrow.

"To a Friend"

You said you cared
But where is the friendship you professed?
Where is the "peace and love" you speak about?
Everything passes through a complete circle—
Thus again the beginning—
So goes it—
It's the same as it used to be,
The same lies and the same hurt;
Again you tear little pieces from me
Day by day—
Sometimes you glue the pieces together
But they don't seem to stick.
Next time remember
"Fragile; Handle with Care"
Before you begin to tear.
Then retreat back into your selfishness
Or
Carelessness
Or
Whatever sustains you
As you kick the dirt
Smiling that innocent smile.

The Seasons

Facing Spring

I am alien

To the patch of green

And sky of splendid blue

Which covers springtime air.

Strangers with ashen faces

Speak in muted tongues.

Seeking warmth of my winter coat,

I watch people jog about—

I am trapped

In the mud of rainy nights.

Spring

On a twisted night of abortive Spring,
Tortured pieces
Of my brain
Produce inarticulate sounds
To a splintering wind
Whose ears
Are numb
And a cardboard tree
Whose limbs
Are torn.
My eyelids snap shut to obliterate
The lingering memories hidden
In a
Soul
Now
DEAD.

Summer's End

Ashen August days

Weave a murky web

Of greying leaves

And stagnant air.

And she, her jaundiced face

And idle legs,

Has lost the promise

Of gleaming rainbows

To face the death

Of an early Fall.

Wilting Flowers

After the sweltering sun
Killed summer's roses,
Only a black moon remained,
Crooked in its cradle,
Smiling smugly upon
The fools who tried to hold
Their transient eternity together,
And upon those who floated
Through ephemeral dreams,
Unaware of the eternal refuse
That lay beneath
The sea of tranquility.

Winter

I need you so much more
On these grey, frigid days,
When snow hangs in its noose
Threatening, ever threatening.
For don't you know
That I have walked
Past street corners
When the wind unwrapped my coat
And pierced my toes?
It's the toes that need warmth most,
For they are small and delicate—
I need you to melt the ice
Or at least to hold my hand
When walking past street corners
Before I SLIP.

Blue January

Blue January stayed

Like an aftertaste in my mouth,

Like the torn Christmas wrappings

Under a wilting tree.

The crackling cold

Seemed terminal,

Freezing all my ripened resolutions

That had nowhere to go.

Ivory snow

Turned to oozing slush,

As Winter traveled onward

Promising only sterile Spring ...

Love

To Steven

Teach me what I need to know
So that I can be whole—
Give me the warmth I need
So that I can feel the sun
And touch His golden fingers.
Let me hold you
So that I can give love—
Don't be afraid;
I will not chain you to the ground
Nor hurt you—
Let me feel
Let me touch
Let me strengthen—
If you can't let me,
Don't look back
Just walk—
But remember how I tried.

To Steven II

We touch and holdthemomentstogether
Without knowing
Each other's names.
There are things I want to give
But can't.
Fear, I guess
And the wall
Numbs my fingers.
You say you felt a feeling once;
Why didn't you tell me then,
Instead of now, after it has passed
Into an endless abyss?
That's easier, I guess—
But remember
That the leaves turn
From gold to brown
And they'll wither in your hands
Leaving the trees naked, crying for clothes.

You are the only meaning in my life,

The only days I care about—

The only one I want to be with—

For life for me begins with you—

You are my ocean and my stars

The sun that lights my way ...

I will come to you softly

To give you all the secrets of my soul I have inside

And touch you where no one else has touched you so far.

Your love has enriched my life

And brought to me a new release,

Lacing my days with magic.

I need you always by my side,

To make me whole,

To make my life complete,

To make my life divine,

As only you can do.

I need to love you,

To learn the riches of your body,

And offer all I have to give.

You're all I want, all I need,

So I will hold you in my heart.

You make each moment so special,

Times I'll capture like photos in my heart,

Always to remember—

You've made me see life with new-born eyes

And speak words of love with new meaning.

You've put new colors in my life

That will outshine the greys

And brought new music

That we sing together.

You are everything to me,
My daylight, my starshine,
The rainbows of my skies—
You have calmed my storms, eased my pain,
And touched my heart.
You are my golden magnet,
The piece that fits my broken puzzle,
As you ease me gently
Into your warm embrace.
You are my complement,
The part I can't ignore;
How can they say
Our love is just a dream?

I love you more than I can say,
And want to be everything to you.
I want to share your smiles
And dry your tears,
Awaking to your morning kisses,
Enfolded in your arms,
As love weaves us closer together
With each passing day.
Without being told,
We know.
For what does life mean
Without love?
Me without you.
A broken shell.

You're the heart and soul of me,

The biggest part I can't ignore,

Bringing all the sunshine of my days,

All the hope inside my dreams.

We're no good without each other,

Like plants without the stems.

You have given life to me,

Flooding me with love.

As I hope I've done for you.

You know I'll never leave you,

The only one I'll ever love.

I cannot live without you, my darling,

For you're the biggest part of me,

The part that makes me whole.

We fit well together,

As you cradle me in your arms

And our hearts beat in unison.

We form a perfect picture,

And will always be together.

We have the greatest love

That blends our lives together.

I could never love you more than I do,

Or need you more deeply than I do.

Loving you is so easy,

Like breathing springtime air.

You are my solace when things go wrong,

Brightness where skies are dark.

Loving you has made me love life,

And sense the wonders of its joys.

I celebrate you

For the way you love me

And ask for nothing in return.

I celebrate your eyes,

As they looked at mine

Without restraint or shame.

I celebrate your body and soul

For letting me wrap myself around you

And find your warmth.

I celebrate you

For showing me how to love you in return

And making my life divine.

You have a way about you

That shows me I can't live without you,

For you love me

In a way that No one else ever has.

You touch me gently,

Then bring my passions

To new highs.

You stay by my side

In ways I can't ignore,

As you ignite a flame

That burns throughout my heart.

You enhance my life in every way,

But most of all,

I love the way you love me.

Mystical Night

On that mystical night
Of shimmering darkness
We were paralyzed
By futile feelings
We could not control.
And dreamed unspoken dreams
Of magical days of communion
As the sweetness of musical notes
Rippled in the blackness—
When the last drop of wine
Had evaporated with the hours
And the candles' light had flickered
We knew that we had left
Those glowing flames behind
And as you caressed me
I could feel the pain
Flow beneath your fingertips.

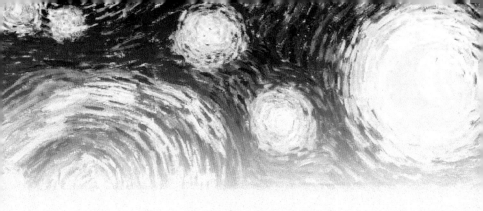

A Special Night

Perhaps it was the moon,

More brilliant and gleaming

In its splendor

That made me want to capture the night

And put it in my pocket

To hold the memories you have brought me ...

In the stillness of the night I found your strength

And then I knew the magic of your love.

I'm so in love with you,

The highlight of my life.

You make holidays out of my everydays,

Special days of ordinary ones,

And are my reason for living.

You make me feel brand new.

A way I've never felt before.

I've never known love like this before.

And know now

That we were meant to be together!

Love
Lost

Just a thought for all the kids and the Freds of the World

I have tried

to make you love life—

And I have tried

to bring you

the gift of joy—

I have given of myself

and can give no more—

You have drained

the life from me

by your indifference

and now only an empty shell

floats beneath the sea.

To Fred

Sleep peacefully, my darling

For I know I have disturbed

The tranquility of your soul

By stirring those flickering embers

so long ago consumed by coldness—

So sleep restfully, my darling

For that will quell the spark of desire

That you have denied me,

And you can always say

That I was just a dream.

On Contemplating A Disability

Once again – To Fred

Now that you've seen
My pitted scars,
Limpid blood,
Imbedded imperfections,
And
Realized that life with me
Tastes not only of crimson wine
But also of parched plums
And is marked
Not only by bouncing balloons
But also of twisted trees.
Knowing this,
Can you still hold me
With the same hands?
If you find yourself leaving,
Walk fast
Without looking back,
For flight lets you forget
All you left behind—

I Cannot See You

I cannot see you
Just as I cannot bear
To look upon
The withering leaves
Whispering in the wind
To their dead lovers.
Nor can I bear
To see the sibilant share
Drowning the drunken fools
Who frolicked in the frothy spray
Who tried to walk upon the whoring waves.
No, I cannot see you,
For you shall pass
Into a parade of plentiful nights
And a mirage of memorable morns
Without me
And without remembering
Our joyous springs
And without knowing
The pain I bear.

An Orange Candle

I lit the candle again tonight

that I had lit with you

for the first time

on the consummate night

when you taught me how to light a match—

But only this time,

its use was to provide light

in a treacherous storm

that I had to face ... alone.

Now all I have

are orange drippings of wax,

smoky cinders of wood

and a window cracked by thunder.

Someday I'll Write A Poem For You

Someday I'll write a poem for you

Speaking all the buried feelings in my soul;

Lines I could not say to you,

Aborted songs I could not sing—

Songs about the colors of the day,

Mottled days of sun and clouds—

Oh, someday I'll write a poem for you

So you will know of all you gave to me.

Rendezvous

Was it I who brought the frost
That froze our hands
And chilled our speech?
Meeting as two strangers meet by chance,
We spoke about the weather,
Pretending we'd never been together.
Surrounded by the jagged ice,
We closed our shades to morning light
And hid beneath the formal clouds
Of muted fears and endless shrouds.
Smothered in trite trivialities,
We failed to penetrate
Our shivering shields or
Spur dormant feelings,
Then parted
To the foreign lands from whence we'd come,
Never knowing
Or caring
Which one of us it was
Who brought the frost.

Loss

Thus the dream fades

Into butt-ends of

Half-smoked cigarettes

And rancid coffee grinds.

All that is left to do

Is to read a legacy

Of suicide poems

While sitting near a yellow flame

That flickers to the ashes

Of the hope you left me.

Not even the fire provides warmth

For feelings smothered by the cold,

Now numb with passivity.

Loneliness

Loneliness

You were there to read between the lines

And see my fire.

You heard the anger

Bursting in my soul.

Maybe you cared enough to see

What no one else ever did.

You told me of my worth

And self-importance.

Still, I can't seem to find my star

Or fill the spaces

When all have gone their way,

Leaving me to sweep the ashes.

Lonely Days

Days without you
Seem like lonely years
That go on interminably,
When empty parts of my soul
Cry out for you.
My body hungers for your touch,
As I need you so very much—
I can only feel complete
When you're near,
Or at least when I can hear
The music of your voice.
I'll try to hold on
And grasp the inner strength
You've infused me with
Through the love you've gently given—
I'll hold on and face the lonely days
'Til you tire of me,
But I can't bear it if you do!

My Radio

The commercial said
"Find a love and share some Canada Dry"
So I
Bought some and sat on a bench
But no one
Came
To share it with me.
So I
Drank it all
And ALL
I got was gas
And I burped—alone.
Then they played
"I Never Promised You a Rose Garden."
But all I wanted
Was a little petal
And ALL
I got was a thorn
And I cried—alone.

Blue Room

I need someone in my blue room,

When it's three o'clock in the morning

In my soul.

I need someone to push the clouds away,

Or at least to help me try.

I squint through shadows

That dim my soul

When thunder rips the skies

And tears the flowers.

Help me face the dawn,

Should it break

Against the ashen sky.

Lone Traveler

Through these deserted woods,
A lone traveler stalks,
Listening to the howling wind,
Searching the sky
For some star to light his way.
Entangled in the silken web
A spider has just weaved,
He flounders,
Then T
       R
         I
           P
             S
On a splintered log he overlooked.
He cries to cardboard trees
And
Rotting leaves
But it is not heard.
No, no one is there to listen
To the moan of the traveler
As he rises clumsily,
Brushes the hardened mud from his pants
And passes, unnoticed, into the Autumn night.

Despair

Emptiness

She didn't know

What it was

That took

The sun

From her soul,

The beauty from her pen,

The joy from her thoughts

And left her barren.

Perhaps it was

The impenetrable darkness,

The clouds she could not move.

But still,

Gazing from the window,

She dreamed of

Those golden days

That brought her happiness

And dried her tears.

During ephemeral, celestial nights
We reach out and grasp each other's hands,
For then we were possessed by
Exotic passions
And
Crimson desires—
But
During stark afternoons
We stand staunchly
With hands at sides
And eyes
Coldly indifferent,
Obliterating the memories
Of nights gone before.

Dreams

I don't remember anymore
what I wanted—
There were so many things—
But now all I have is
a broken bottle of
fractured dreams ...
I don't remember anymore
who I am—
I was so many things once
But now all I am is
a shattered vase of
withered dreams.

Nightmare

Bursting moments of blackness

Split my brain,

Descend it into madness,

Crack my skull,

Until

It can no longer be mended,

Until reality

Is a nightmare

Of splintered people

And music that blasts all to bits.

Plunged into this cell of bursting suns,

I can no longer take the heat.

Silent House

Living in a house cloaked in whispers,

She dives against doors marked

"DO NOT ENTER."

Her brain is split by bloody claws

And legs are crushed by stagnant air.

She fears the span of time

In this spider-ridden shack

Where no one hears her silent words

That twist her mouth

And tie her tongue.

She cannot find the key and screams

"A cup of coffee, please!"

It seemed so easy,

Just to toss the lyrics of my life,

The verses of my soul,

Into the mailbox.

To pass away the pages that I'd written,

To let others peer into my mind

Seemed such an easy task,

Until I realized what I'd done—

The day grows older and I am cold.

Pregnant

A silent poet,
She walks,
Pregnant with verse,
Unbeknownst to all—
Her mind is bursting
With chaotic images,
That loosely swim
In flaming crimson
And muted greys.
She cannot conceive
Her frigid verse
Which fades into
Her stillborn mind
And cracks her skull.

Struggle

The soul wrenches in anguish,

Struggles to be free,

To permeate yours,

Needing its strength and freedom

Fire ignites parched ashes

Bleeding an arid heart,

Raising a deadened brain

to consciousness.

Sun, nourish the body,

Strengthen its roots,

Heal its pain.

Quandary

Sudden gusts of icy wind

On Indian Summer days

Mock us in their warnings

These days—

These days I feel the signs

Of passing years—

Grey shadows 'neath my eyes

That happened quickly—

SO many things

That I forgot to do—

Still, lines to write

Will bring new hope,

Won't they?

Aging

I don't remember
When it was I grew so old.
After all,
I'm only twenty-eight
Going on fifty.
Looking in the mirror is always traumatic
Eyes deadened by bitterness
And
Lips cracked by cynicism
Stare back at me.
Stripped bare of all dreams,
I stand naked before you,
Wondering where I strayed off course.
I fought so hard
To light your way.
Knowing that I failed,
I stand here, helpless,
Wondering
When it was I grew so old.

Hope

New Hope

Although I never met you face to face,
In your way, you gave me hope,
Where there was none,
Confidence where there was little.
I laid bare my soul to you,
The most difficult thing I've ever done,
And you never laughed, as I feared you might.
I thought I was NO ONE,
But you've shown me how wrong I was.
I thought I lived by chance,
With nothing to show for my life,
But you showed me that I have some worth,
In my own small way,
Although it may not be enough
For those more cynical than you.

I thought my dreams were like a broken vase

Until you came along

And promised me new tomorrows—

You gently mended my dreams

And have let me give to you in return.

Most of all,

You've taught me that

Love doesn't hurt so very much, after all

And now all I want to do is hold you—tight!

Your love has brought me so much comfort,

so much assurance,

For you are a Rock, a pillar of Strength,

Solid, yet so soft and tender — Restored my Hope

And made me feel alive in your caress —

I celebrate you,

For you have shared your life and love with me,

and held back the stars to light my way.

Somehow you've made me Believe again

When you brought shining stars

That pushed the clouds

Behind a melon moon.

In a special way,

The early sunrise

Became my friend

And I know

The flowers will not wilt—

Not for a while, anyway—

I will remember these days

That only poems can capture.

Clearing

She knew only how to sing the blues

Until

He brought her laughter,

Softly, with a pen, some smiles, a glow—

He cleansed her grief

And left a rainbow

Past the storm

'Til she could see the daybreak.

Death

Little Boy

He was so young,

Too young

And yet he learned

Of the inevitability of death.

Never again would he hear

The old man's delicious fables

And sage stories.

And he learned that the salad days of summer

Pass into

The ripening days of Fall.

And he learned, too,

That we are only here

To be hurt a little more each moment

By the frigid winds of Winter.

World

The world collapsed today
Not with splurging fireworks,
Not with screaming stars,
Not with bursting suns—
No.
The world collapsed today
With
A grumbling groan,
A whispering passion
Leaving
Floating scum,
Stinking sewage
And
ME
ALONE
With hands stretched to
NOTHINGNESS
And lips parted
Uttering speechless sounds.

War

After the destruction,

Only a pleading child remained

reaching out his hands

Into the dust,

yearning for the broken bird

that had fallen helplessly;

But the bird died on that day,

and the child, alone,

crumbled a little more each moment

until only the dust remained.

Au Revoir

Au Revoir

Numbed by the stillness
Of the crimson room
And changed by the different paths
Their lives had taken,
They vainly tried
To describe endless days
In the space of an hour.
They spoke of flooding rains
And withered leaves
Rather than zealous dreams
And
Urgent needs.
With the aging of the hour,
They learned that rains
Wash away so much,
Leaving no rainbow at the end.
As the last flame flickered,
They pretended
Nothing had changed
And
Lightly said "Goodbye."

Finale

Bury all the foolish poems,
Written with the lyrics of the wind,
Poems for paths that never cross
And wine never sipped—
No more celebrations
Of moments never shared—
Stash away the party hats,
Sweep the china off the floor;
Wipe away the tears never shed;
Know of all you could have had,
All you killed,
Know of all I had to give,
Know why I didn't.

There is no one here now,
No one to help me drink
The left-over wine
Of grey yesterdays
And blue tomorrows.
Tangled here in silken cobwebs
Of drifting clouds,
I Sing In Silence

Afterword

Summer of '42 in '71

We emerged from the cinema,
shivering quietly.
The movie had captured our minds.
And I didn't have to reach out
to know you were still there beside me.
We emerged trembling speechlessly
because we had nothing to say.
Words washed in a union of thought.
And we walked without speaking,
listening to the night,
smelling the hot air and roses
as we silently strolled along palm-lined streets
far from the interference of traffic.
And then we sat in the car,
sleepily tuned to Schubert
and gazed softly out the window
afraid to speak
that we might puncture
the vibrantly still completeness
of that August night.
We went our own ways,
but I shall long remember
you, the music, the movie
and the summer of '71.

~ Gerald Weinberg
Robyn's Friend,

You were there when I needed you
as you still are
as I still need you.
Although I do not love you
(whatever love is anyway)
I feel something for you
not because you listened
nor because you cared
but
because you are you.
And all that is good
(when so little exists)
is in you.
Your touch has washed
bitterness
and loneliness
away
and in its stead
you have given
of yourself
(as I believe you always will)
and you have given
hope
(where there was none)
and you have pulled me up
(when I sank in self-pity)
Although I do not love you
I
Feel
Something

~ Gerald Weinberg
Robyn's Friend,
August 9, 1971

"How's My Little Girl?"

My eyes are full of tears...
how long has it been—how many years...
the tending—the love—the caring.
I hear the sounds of my heart — tearing,
crumbling into hundreds of pieces
causing such pulsating pain,
                    dulling my brain.
Nothing will ever be the same.
Surely not as I intended.
In hospital I left my little girl,
only to bring home a broken doll
            that can never be mended.

~ Estelle Taradash
Robyn's Mom

Remembering Robyn

I loved her Smile and Humor and her easy Laughter.
It will reverberate in my heart and soul forever after.
Her jokes were so funny — her disposition usually sunny,
And when she received a greeting card she always asked
"Did they send any Money?"

When her Doctors inquired —"how's your appetite?"
She would say "I'm on a seafood diet—
when I see food I eat!"
It always got a laugh — It was like a little treat.
She knew every commercial on TV,
From dogs singing "There Ain't No Bugs on Me."
And "When You're Here — You're Family"
To "Come Hungry — Leave Happy"
and other Jingles that were snappy.
But before saying goodnite and putting out the light,
Her favorite line was—"Live From New York—
It's Saturday Night!"
As I tucked her in bed — I always said,
"I Love you, Robyn — I'll see you Tomorrow."
She said "I love you Ma, I'll see you tomorrow."

I could never imagine the tragedy to follow
That brought so much pain and unbearable sorrow.
I cradled her and kissed her as she drew her final breath;
Never did I dream I would be witness to her death.
She went as Peaceful as a Dove
She took nothing with her but my love.
And I hope when God welcomes her that an angel sings,
For Robyn was my hero —
She was the Wind Beneath my Wings.

~ Estelle Taradash
Robyn's Mother

8/26/82

To dear Robyn:

To evil eye of fate do not
                surrender!
Keep up the fight with will
              and brain.
In time you'll reap the
           satisfaction's grandeur

For earthly sojourned not,
            IN vain!

        Respectfully

        Harry Pires.

Evergreen Poems

Harry Pines

Exposition Press   *Smithtown, New York*

The Puzzle

Multiple Sclerosis is a puzzle that has perplexed medical science since it was first described by the French neurologist Charcot in 1868. The disease affects the central nervous system and can, to varying degrees, interfere with the transmission of nerve impulses throughout the brain, spinal cord and optic nerves.

Since identification, MS has been the subject of intense, world-wide research but still its cause and cure remain elusive.

A simple explanation is conveyed by the term itself. Sclerosis is a Greek word meaning "hardened tissue or scars" and multiple means many. Recurring episodes of MS can cause many scars to appear in the central nervous system as a result of the breakdown of the myelin, the insulating material that covers the nerve fibres. This can result in impairment of motor, sensory and cognitive functions to a greater or lesser extent.

But multiple describes other aspects of what is often a frustratingly unpredictable disease. Episodes can occur at varying time intervals affecting different areas of the central nervous system. There is no one symptom that indicates the presence of MS. No single test can establish an accurate diagnosis.

It can be benign—in rare cases apparently disappearing altogether after one or two episodes. Or it can progress steadily over many years, bringing about a slow deterioration in an individual's capabilities.

We do not yet understand why some people are susceptible and others are not.

The List

Neil Cavuto, News Anchor

Betty Cuthbert, Australian Athlete

Joan Didion, American Writer

Jacqueline du Pre, Cellist

Annette Funincello, Actress/Singer

Lola Falana, Singer/Dancer/Poet

Dino Ferrari, Ferrari Automobiles

Terri Garr, Actress

Marianne Gingrich, Ex-Wife of Newt Gingrich

Carlos Hathcock, Marine Sniper

Barbara Jordan, Congresswoman, Activist

David "Squiggy" Lander, Actor

Alan Osmond, Singer

Richard Pryor, Comedian/Actor

Fraser Robinson III, Michele Obama's Father

Ann Romney, Wife of Mitt Romney

Anne Rowling, Mother of Author J.K. Rowling

Kelly Sutton, Race Car Driver

Robyn Taradash, Poet

Clay Walker, Country Western Singer

Stephen White, Author

Montel Williams, Television Host

16655098R00060

Made in the USA
Charleston, SC
04 January 2013